Sting Like A Bee

Charlotte Ridgewell

BookLeaf
Publishing

India | USA | UK

Presentation by *BookLeaf Publishing*

Web: www.bookleafpub.com

E-mail: info@bookleafpub.com

ISBN: 9789358319682

First edition 2023

This is for anyone that is struggling, and also those that have survived - you've got this. Step by step and day by day. It can get better.

ACKNOWLEDGEMENT

I know usually this section is used for thanking those that helped in the actual book making process but since there aren't many of those (oh hi Bookleaf Publishing, I'm grateful for you!) I'm going to take the opportunity to thank the people in my life.

I cant name everyone specifically but to anyone that has given me a smile, given me their time, made me laugh, given me a hug or picked me up on the days I've felt alone (even if it's not obvious to the naked eye) - you are unsung heroes and I appreciate you more than you know. And equally to those who have shared the good moments - thank you for the memories. You've all made me the person I am today.

Thank you to my Mum and Step-Dad (who is basically the real deal, for all he does for me) and to Simon and Hannah - four of the only people who have always been by my side.

And thank you to my lucky number five. You gave me the push to do this - through all my wobbles and stress head days, you're still in my corner cheering me on. Thank you for forever challenging me to do better and holding my hand through it all. You're truly a powerful force to be reckoned with.

I love you all so much.

Afraid

How can you start to word things, when you're
too afraid to try,
Afraid you might upset someone, or even make
them cry.

How can you hold on tightly, to the one you love
the most,
Afraid that if you let them go, they'll soon
become a ghost.

How can you give your heart away, afraid to
start anew,
How can you love another when you have no
faith in you.

How can you wave goodbye to them and wait
another day,
When frozen and afraid you are that they'll be
taken away.

How can you promise them the world, when
scared of what it holds,
Afraid that when you turn your back, everybody
folds.

How can you fight the demons in the corners of
your mind,
Afraid your love will run away at the sight of
what they find.

How can you move on forward, afraid you aren't
enough,
Afraid they'll see right through you when you
act all big and tough.

How can you beat the monsters that set up camp
and stayed,
When every second of every hour, you're just so
damn afraid.

Before

I was alone and grieving for a love I never lost,
You saw your chance, at pitiful cost.

You swept in quietly, a friend of new,
But you quickly made it all about you.

I cried for my present and you cried for your
past,
How could I have known I'd fall so fast.

Long car conversations and hands to hold,
I'd never have pictured you so cruel and cold.

You lit up my days, and held me at night,
You gave me the strength I needed to fight.

You built me up so you were all that I knew,
How could I know, you'd break me down too?

So loving, so caring, so all over me,
The anger, the drama, I tried not to see.

The cracks in the mask, that soon enough fell,
But by then, darling, you'd dragged me to hell.

I was yours to play with, torment and control,
You smiled at me while you dug my hole.

You knew I'd go down, fight for your name,
Its the way I was raised - to take the blame.

I defended, I grovelled, and all for what?
For torture, for pain, for diddly squat.

I let you abuse me, scream and fight,
I let you believe you were always right.

I let the others think 'little miss perfect' was
real,
Because how could they understand how you
really made me feel?

You slowly did me just as he did you,
but really though, was that even true?

I believed you back then, my heart struck a
chord,
But really, be real, you were just bored.

Tales of heartbreak and destructive abuse,
Or maybe you hated that he cut you loose.

I thought you were honest, and for you I'd die,
But it turns out, baby, you were living a lie.

So I guess I did die, but only inside,
At the loss of a lover, the narcissist's faux hide.

Ghosting

I've been ghosting people for a while now.

Only to me the term is a little different.

I've been floating on through my days -
Unaware of what I'm really doing,
Where I'm going,
Who I really am,
Or what my purpose is.

I have minimal contact with humans,
And when I do its only the ones who *really*
see me that respond.

I observe everything,
But I never really have the chance to join in.

Its loneliness wrapped up in an ethereal blanket,
As I work out what I need to do to fade between
this world and the next.

You didn't

If ever I was asked to sum up in two words,
Our relationship, the hurt, the outright absurd.
I'd hand them "you didn't" for all it entails,
But for you I'll write down the gory details.

You didn't stay loyal,
You didn't stay home,
You didn't stay close,
When I felt alone.

You didn't really love me,
You didn't really care,
You didn't give a fuck if I was even there.

You didn't mind gas-lighting,
You didn't drop the mask,
Until I was sucked into your glorious farce.

You didn't assure me,
You didn't tell the truth,
You didn't falter when I handed you proof.

You didn't trust me,
You didn't believe,
You didn't have a problem

Putting me down on my knees.

You didn't worry for my mental health,
You didn't worry for nowt but yourself.
You didn't worry about getting caught,
You didn't worry what anyone thought.

You didn't stop hurting me,
You didn't stop to think,
You didn't mind pushing more,
When I was at the brink.

So yes, if they asked me, I sure would tell,
Of the times you'd belittle me, curse and yell,
How you'd hurt me, betray me, sneer and lie,
How you pushed me to the point of wanting to
die.
I'd explain how I almost came down to your
level,
But stopped when I realised I'd danced with the
devil.

Gaslighting

Going round in circles, making me feel like I'm
insane,
Anxiety at an all time high, panic attacks on the
sidelines.
Suggesting that I'm paranoid, crazy or dramatic,
Letting me know that everyone else thinks so
too.
Implying I did something that was actually all
you,
Giving ridiculous excuses and accusations to
avoid accountability.
Handing me false promises and dreams we'll
never reach,
Telling me something is 'just a joke', when we
both know it's not.
Informing me that my feelings are invalid,
Not letting me get a word in edgeways, defences
at a new high,
Getting me to give up the fight, you win.

Barely

You changed me.
But you didn't do it softly, or kindly,
or gently, or all at once.
No, no.
You did it slowly, carefully over time,
Getting inside of my mind before pulling the rug
from my feet in one foul swoop of an end game.
You beat my spirit until it was black and blue.
You kissed my lips just to rip the skin from
them.
You touched all of the places nobody got to -
just to carve your name and leave it to bleed.
You held me close just so others couldn't.
You projected all of the ugliest parts of yourself
and scarred my skin with them.
You awakened traits I hadn't felt in a long time -
anger, worry, suspicion, jealousy - and let me
cast them upon people.
You changed me.
And then you left the body there.
Barely warm.
Barely human.
Barely breathing.
Barely holding on.

During

I gave you my time, every ounce I could muster,
You gave me excuses, all in a fluster.

I gave you my heart, it was yours to handle,
You took yours away, like dimming a candle.

I gave you my love, no questions asked,
You gave some back, albeit masked.

I gave you my care, a shoulder, a hand,
You slipped through the cracks, like grains of
sand.

I gave you forgiveness, for all of your sins,
You took my kindness for weakness, your little
wins.

I gave you my loyalty, served it up on a plate,
You gave me the stories you loved to create.

I gave you my freedom, threw out the key,
You did what you wanted, no worry for me.

I gave you my trust, but you went and broke it,
Yet I kept coming back, it's not in me to quit.

I gave you my secrets, believed you would stay,
You hid yours from me before walking away.

Understood?

If you don't understand why she:

Flinches if you move too fast when you're close to her...

Breaks down after the slightest disagreement...

Puts up her walls when things get too real...

Doubts the truth in your words...

Questions the motive behind everything...

Revolves all of her boundaries around the one that came before you...

Then be grateful that you don't.

And if you'll never understand any of it? Leave her be, you're not the one for her. Understood?

Obliviate

I know there will come a day when there are no
more reminders of you in my life:

The clothes you bought me will wear through
and get tossed out.

The perfume you sprayed everywhere will fade
from my room.

The photos will be taken down, in favour of
new, better memories.

I wont think twice when I drive past the places
we used to go.

I wont want you with me when I'm planning the
next adventure.

I wont feel the need to question anything and
everything.

I know all of this. And yet I'm not sure if the
idea terrifies me or excites me.

Either way it gives me butterflies that feel more
like woodpeckers.
Peck, peck peck,
Until there's nothing left.

Four Letter Words

Hate is a strong 4 letter word,
Probably one of the most powerful there is.
And yet we use it so casually day to day:
We hate traffic. We hate vegetables. We hate our
jobs. We hate noisy neighbours.

Love is a wholesome 4 letter word,
Yet we struggle to truly and honestly convey it
to the people around us:
We love laughing. We love our friends. We love
our family. We love being loved.

Can't is a lazy 4 letter word,
And we impose it so negatively on ourselves:
We can't do this. We can't say that. We can't eat
this. We can't wear that.

Don't is a warning of a 4 letter word,
And we use it carelessly sometimes without
realising:
Don't touch that. Don't worry about it. Don't go
there. Don't get close to that person.

Time is a fleeting 4 letter word,

Before we know it it has run away with us and
all we are left with is excuses:
We don't have time to call our parents back. We
didn't catch the bus on time. We don't have time
to play games. We didn't have time to read a
bedtime story.

Four little letters can have such an impact, but
here's the thing:

Maybe if we spread hate a little less, and love a
little more, we would realise that not one person
on this earth has the right to tell us what we can
and cant be. We don't need to have everything
mapped out, we can just take it one step at a
time with purity in our hearts, making time for
the thing's that matter most along the way

Wonder

Sometimes I wonder how it feels to be you,
Is it dark? Does it hurt? Is it cold?

I wonder what you tell them to draw them in,
What is it that takes a hold?

I wonder how you truly see me,
Do you love me? Hate me? Or worse?

I wonder how you'll paint me to future loves,
An abuser? A blessing? A curse?

I wonder how it could have been if you'd been
honest,
Would I be happy? Sad? Afraid?

I often wonder who will be next,
Will they notice they're being played?

I wonder if you'll come running back,
Most likely, we never learn.

But mostly I wonder why I wonder,
 when it's no longer my concern.

Natural Disaster

I know that a storm is coming.
Only I don't know if I'll be at its eye,
Or buried in its wake.

I know the tide will rise, just to retreat again,
And the winds of change will blow me down.
But not forever, mind.

I know the tornado in my head will rage,
It could take cars and planes and trains with it.
But will it take us away too?

I know the tsunami will destroy the home we
built,
And the landslide will take our neighbours.
But stand strong, my love.

The ground will shake, earth will quake,
Volcanoes may spew lava upon all we've ever
known.
But as they say - a phoenix will rise.

I know that when it clears, all will be clear.
But who the survivors are, and who will perish,
I'm deeply unsure.

Sting Like A Bee

There was a time when you said,
You were likened to a bee,
A sting in your tail, a flap in your wings,
For all the world to see.

Bright and bumbling, full of life,
I thought I saw it too,
The light and breezy, take it easy,
None of that was you.

I took the ride, through rough terrain,
Convinced I had real love,
Me, the nectar to your crop,
Until you dropped me from above.

But you my dear, are not a bee,
Not even close it would seem.
Your fuzz is thinning, buzz not winning,
No longer part of a team.

You, my love, are more of a wasp,
Threatened and stinging for fun,
I wish I had listened, way back then,
When they all told me to run.

After

I always wondered how I would cope with the
loss of you,
I thought I would struggle but actually, since
then I have…

Visited 10 different countries - ticking off the list
slowly but surely.

Sung my heart out to approximately 7,800 songs
in the car. That's around 27,300 minutes of
uninterrupted, joyous moments.

Watched around 1,277 hours of the shows I want
to watch, no complaints or argumentative
distractions.

Joined 3 support groups - like-minded people
whose stories have helped bring me back down
to earth.

Had around 2,600 conversations where I'm not
watching over my shoulder, afraid of the
backlash.

Spent around 208 days seeing my loved ones, trying new things and enjoying myself instead of waiting in all day just to be let down.

Written 21 poems to publish my first ever book - a new step in the direction I want to climb.

Met 1 person that made it all worth it.

Untitled

I used to chase approval.

I used to want people to like me and it felt like the end of the world if I had even the slightest disagreement with someone.

I would bend until I broke, for everybody.
I would do whatever they asked, when they asked, because I thought that's what I was supposed to do.
Even when the sentiment wasn't returned;
Even when I was at the point of mental and physical exhaustion.
I thought that's what I had to do to keep love - to keep my friends.

But it turns out it doesn't work like that.
If someone loves you for you, its that simple.
No bending. No breaking. Just pure, mutual understanding.
Having each-others back, no matter what, not stabbing each-other in them.

Looking back on who I used to be (compared to who I am today)

I can 100% say I would rather have nobody (or very few people) than to be surrounded by fakes.
I don't chase anybody anymore.
Nobody is worth breaking yourself for.
And I was most certainly lonelier surrounded by those people than I ever am now.

Some of you aren't ready for that revelation.
You know deep down, but you don't want to accept it.
I was you once.
It took me too many years to see it.
But maybe one day I'll see you on the other side of the vipers pit.
When you crawl out bloody and bruised, awakening from the hell you've been stuck in, and realisation dawns on you - I'll be there to hold your hand and patch the wounds.

Because that's who I've always been.

Humanity

I lost faith in humanity, somewhere along the
way,
I couldn't narrow down a year, nor month, nor
week, nor day.

It could have been a sunny Sunday, or rainy
Monday blues,
All I know is losing faith isn't something I
would choose.

It takes your brightest moments, it steals your
happy days,
I'm hoping that this loss in faith will only be a
phase.

It narrows your suspicions, makes everyone a
threat,
Lately there has been no trust in anyone I've
met.

It questions your intentions, throws shade on all
you see,
It makes you wonder, above all else - "why, oh
why me?"

Just as it got frightening, I noticed there was you,
Then came the possibility of some kind of faith anew.

So thank you for this blessing, for showing me the way,
But most of all thank you for telling me you'll stay.

Thank you just for being you, a ray of sunshine in the wrong,
For showing me I don't always have to be this strong.

I lost faith in humanity somewhere along the way,
Then came your voice, out from the dark: "It'll all be okay."

Dandelions

I watched from a distance,
As you grew and changed,
Through all your seasons.
I didn't know you'd done the same.

You made observations,
Quiet and calculated,
Working out how best to help me bloom.

You planted the seeds,
And from my bruises, flowers grew.
You made me believe I could reach for the sun
again,
Even on the cloudiest of days.

You helped me move forward,
The transformation from solid and weedy,
To light and free.

You only wanted what was best for me,
From the soil I rooted myself in,
Down to the thoughts I watered myself with
daily.

And if there should come a day,

That you blow me away,
I will let you.
Because, honestly?
You already did.

Thank You

Thank you to the friends,
Though they remain a few.
The ones who picked me up,
When I didn't know what to do.

Thank you for understanding,
And walking me through the dark.
Thank you for holding my hand,
And leaving your own mark.

Thank you for your patience,
And all the times you tried.
The times you sat beside me,
While I moped and sulked and cried.

Thank you for the laughter,
And for keeping me afloat.
For all the words of encouragement,
I used as an armoured coat.

Thank you for always having my back,
And for never letting me drown.
Even on the days,
that meant you acting like the clown.

Thank you just for being you,
And for making me aware.
That not everybody is out to hurt me,
Some will love and care.

Thank you for being a part of my life,
From the bottom of my heart,
And here's to hoping, with everything in me,
We get that brand new start.

An Apology To My Collateral Damage

If you got caught between what was fair and
what was right-
Remember, things may not have always been
fair to you when it came to me,
But they were never fair to me either.
I did what I felt was right at the time.

If you got caught up in the crossfire between my
head and my heart,
Then you probably meant a lot to me.
I just couldn't do anything to prove that at the
time,
So I folded instead.

If you got caught between my brain and my
tongue,
When my words were like spitfires in the sky,
I'm sorry I couldn't hold it in,
But it would have been a long time coming.

If you got caught between me and another
person:
Choose them… always choose them,
Because I am second to nobody.

If your loyalty was thrown into question, you know by now that I would jump before I was pushed.
If I walked away - now you know why.

So yes, I am truly sorry,
I never wanted you to be the collateral in my story.
But I will never be as sorry to you now,
As I was to myself back then.
That's what makes me stand by my decisions.
I chose me.
I still choose me.

I loved you & goodbye

If I could turn back the time, I wouldn't change
our path,
I'd just hold on a little tighter, to the times you
made me laugh.
I'd look a little deeper into those beautiful green
eyes,
Get lost in them, then try to ignore the bullshit
and the lies.

I'd grasp a little tighter to the moments you were
'mine',
And try to lengthen out the days we could say
that we were 'fine'.
I'd take your hand and hold it through the happy
and the sad,
I'd wipe your tears and take the blows whenever
you were mad.

I'd take us on more holidays, our own perfect
little place,
I'd spend more hours laid in bed just staring at
your face.
I'd drink the drink, I'd smoke the smoke, do
whatever you want to,

I'd hide away all my concerns so you didn't
have a clue.

I'd watch sunsets and go for drives, I'd do things
couples do,
Just to make them bitter-sweet, so they taste just
like you.
I'd stand up and I'd claim your heart, without an
ounce of fear,
But secrecy was always your preference, wasn't
it, my dear?

I'd listen harder when you spoke, and even when
you'd shout,
I'd try my best to calm you down and find us a
way out.
I'd try to understand your side and view things
how you do,
Even when I know there's nothing left for me
and you.

I'd bite my tongue and hold my breath, whatever
it would take,
I'd remind myself daily of the life that we could
make.
I'd let you tell your tales and lies, though I never
understood,
Just so that I know myself, I did all that I could.

I'd do all this, I'd try my best, but I'd know its
all in vain,
Because destiny mapped out for me the
heartbreak and the pain.
And with that said, I'd take the hit, to spend that
time with you,
Because regardless how false yours may be, my
love was always true.

I say this now because I can, no longer stuck in
fear,
No more pretending and bending to break just to
keep you near.
No more hiding, tucked away and stuck inside
my shell,
No more worrying about the lies that you will
always tell.

No more rose glasses to hide the truth of who
you've always been,
No more concern for other people and how I will
be seen.
I know the truth and that's what counts, it's not
all in my head,
And thankfully no more wishing that I'd wake
up dead.

So no, if I could turn back the clock, I wouldn't
change the end,

Though at the time it meant me losing a lover
and best friend.
To say I'd ever want 'you' back would surely be
a lie,
So sadly all that's left to say is I loved you &
goodbye.

My Lucky Number Five

You Don't even realise what you do, do you?

You love me on the days that I don't even like
myself.
You remind me that my worth is found in those
that care for me, not those that don't.

You make me smile every single day.
Sometimes my cheeks don't know what to do
with themselves because that feeling had been
missing for so long.

You make me laugh, too.
You give as good as you get - with the puns and
innuendos, the inside jokes, and the ability to
clown around just because you enjoy watching
me light up in response.

You hold me in my moments of weakness.
They overcome me sometimes (though they've
been few and far between since you came along)
but when they do strike, I know I have you.

You're so very patient with me.

I have a lot of triggers and trauma I am still battling every day and you take that in your stride even though you weren't the cause of them.
A lesser person would have walked away by now.

You gave me my voice back - in two ways.
You listen to me about every single little thing that goes through my head, happy or sad.
And you listen to me sing in the car without silencing me (I think you actually enjoy it). That was a bigger deal than you'll ever realise.

You make me comfortable and make me feel safe.
You never push me past my boundaries - you let me take things at my own pace, but are also there to help me if I need it.

You support my dreams.
Lets be perfectly honest - if it wasn't for you, I wouldn't even be writing this right now. You push me to do better every day.

You've helped me to grow.
Like a sunflower in the summer sun, stretching up and up, you've made me feel like I can do anything I put my mind to.

Thank you for just being you.
I hope I am/can be all of these things for you
too. One thing is for sure though - your heart is
golden and your intentions are clear, regardless
of your past. You are exactly what I needed.
I think I maybe, kind of, *like* you a lot too.